SUFFOLK
TRANSPORT

ROBERT MALSTER

This book was first published in 1997 by
Sutton Publishing Limited

This edition first published in 2003 by
Lucas Books

Copyright © Robert Malster, 1997

British Library Cataloguing in Publication Data
A catalogue record for this book is available from the
British Library.

ISBN 1 903797 41 1

Typeset in 10/12 Perpetua.
Typesetting and origination by
Sutton Publishing Limited.
Printed in Great Britain by
J.H. Haynes & Co. Ltd, Sparkford.

Title page: A steam road locomotive built by Ransomes Sims & Jefferies at Orwell Works, Ipswich, *c.* 1912. (Ransomes Sims & Jefferies, Ipswich Transport Museum collection)

Exchanging the tablet, a feature of single-line branches. Here a T26 pilots a T19 whose fireman hangs from the cab with the tablet for the section just passed, which he will deposit on the retrieving apparatus; he will then pick up the tablet for the section ahead, fitted in the apparatus in the foreground. (Ipswich Transport Museum)

CONTENTS

The road surface in Lowestoft High Street *c.* 1880 does not appear to be entirely satisfactory, yet the town was one of the first to have its streets paved – about a century before this photograph was taken. The nature of the highways had a considerable influence on transport, particularly when some Suffolk country roads were rendered impassable by heavy rain every winter.

INTRODUCTION

A maritime county with the North Sea on one side and the Fenland on the other, Suffolk has in past centuries depended to a very great extent on sea and river transport both to bring in essential supplies such as coal and to export its products, predominantly those grown on the farms and those turned out by such related industries as malting.

In the west the Fenland waterways radiating from the port of King's Lynn were used to supply Bury St Edmunds, Mildenhall and Brandon once the Lark and the Little Ouse had been made navigable. On the North Sea coast Ipswich was the most significant port, but there were also smaller places such as Woodbridge on the Deben, Orford and Aldeburgh on that river that enjoys two names, Ore and Alde, Southwold on the Blyth and Lowestoft, a town that enjoyed a shipping trade even before its harbour was constructed in the 1830s as part of a grandiose plan to bring seagoing ships upriver to the city of Norwich.

The Waveney was used for trade up to Beccles and Bungay from a very early date, and in the late eighteenth century both the Blyth and the Gipping were made navigable for small vessels. The River Stour, whose horse-hauled lighters have been immortalized by John Constable, had a considerable trade not only in coal and timber inwards but in agricultural produce, malt and flour, and bricks, downriver to the quay at Mistley where cargoes were transhipped to seagoing vessels. John's father, Golding Constable, not only sent flour from his mills in Stour lighters but owned his own sloop, the *Telegraph*, to carry his goods onwards to London.

Water transport was particularly important in a period when roads were less than adequately metalled and tended to be impassable in wet weather. Roads across the claylands of High Suffolk were notorious for their ruts. The turnpiking of main roads from the late seventeenth century onwards brought some improvement, but early photographs show that even at the beginning of the twentieth century the surfacing of many highways left a good deal to be desired.

Travel by road tended to be uncomfortable and tedious even in the relatively short-lived reign of the stagecoach. Indeed, most people travelling between Ipswich and London in the second quarter of the nineteenth century preferred to use the paddle steamer that operated a regular service – except when interrupted by violent weather or accident.

Until the coming of what some have called the 'infernal' combustion engine the horse reigned supreme on the roads and on the farms. Steam engines built by Ransomes at Ipswich, Garretts at Leiston and Burrells just over the county boundary at Thetford in Norfolk played their part in heavy haulage, but they were too large and too heavy for the poor roads of the day and were handicapped by legislation that imposed restrictions on their use.

It was on the railways that steam really came into its own. The earliest schemes for building railways in the county turned out to be no more than elaborate swindles, and when the Eastern Counties Railway ran out of money at Colchester in 1839 it seemed that the arrival in Suffolk of the 'iron road' would be long delayed.

Had it not been for the determination of such men as John Cobbold and his son John Chevallier

Cobbold the eastern part of Suffolk might have been left off the railway map for many years. Their formation of the Eastern Union Railway and the construction of a line from Colchester to Ipswich, followed by extensions to Bury St Edmunds and then to Norwich, ensured that by the end of the 1840s the county was beginning to enjoy the advantages of railway communication.

During the second half of the nineteenth century a network of lines spread across Suffolk, but it was not until the early years of the twentieth century that the final pieces were put into the jigsaw. By the time the Mid-Suffolk Light Railway was being pushed from Haughley out towards Halesworth the railways, which had earlier succeeded in putting some of the waterways out of business, were already finding a certain amount of competition from public road transport.

The earliest bus services were in fact introduced by the Great Eastern Railway Company between Lowestoft and Southwold, Ipswich and Shotley, and Bury St Edmunds and Horringer at almost the same time that Ipswich and Lowestoft corporations were laying out electric tramways in those towns.

In Ipswich the trams were replaced between 1923 and 1926 by electric trolleybuses, a form of public transport much more flexible than the lumbering tramcars. Both Ransomes, Sims & Jefferies at Ipswich and Garretts at Leiston undertook the building of trolleybuses for the Ipswich system and also for many other towns and cities both in Britain and in other parts of the world.

Electric traction has many advantages, even if it suffers from the handicap of requiring overhead lines to carry the current used. In the early days of rural buses the Eastern Counties Road Car Company ran petrol-electric buses which employed the internal combustion engine to generate electricity to power the traction motors.

Diesel power plants have taken over from petrol engines in almost all large vehicles in the past fifty years. It is noteworthy that Dr Rudolf Diesel set up a factory in Ipswich to build oil engines in the second decade of this century, and he was in fact on his way to Ipswich to inspect the plant when he disappeared so mysteriously from the Hook of Holland to Harwich ferry.

This book has been produced in association with the Ipswich Transport Museum, which now occupies premises at Priory Heath built to accommodate the Ipswich Corporation fleet of trolleybuses. Many of the photographs have come from the museum's expanding collection, and the author thanks the museum and in particular Mike Abbott for their willing co-operation in the compilation of the book.

Others have also helped with information and with the loan of photographs. Ken Leighton, of the Ipswich and District Historical Transport Society, has given most valuable help in identifying photographs and compiling captions. David Cleveland and the East Anglian Film Archive have as ever supplied pictures and much encouragement; others the author must especially thank are Ivan Codd, Hugh Moffat, John Wilton, and the staff of Suffolk Record Office.

The Ipswich Transport Museum in the old Ipswich Corporation trolleybus depot in Cobham Road, Ipswich, has the largest collection of transport items in Britain related to one town. All the exhibits were made or used in and around Ipswich, the county town of Suffolk. The museum is open every Sunday and Bank Holiday Monday from April to October and, in August only, every afternoon from Monday to Friday.

BY SEA & RIVER

Lowestoft harbour was constructed c. 1830 as part of a scheme to bring seagoing ships to Norwich. Mutford lock, seen here in a print from a drawing by James Stark, linked the harbour to Oulton Broad and had four sets of gates, necessary because of the different times of high water in the harbour and on the fresh-water side of the lock.

Owned by John Steward Sterry, a Lowestoft coal merchant, the barquentine *Alice Sterry* regularly brought coal from the collieries of the north-east for her owner's coal yard in Commercial Road. She is here being towed into Lowestoft harbour and through the swing bridge by one of the Great Eastern Railway paddle tugs at about the turn of the century.

On the south side of Oulton Broad were maltings from which malt was taken to the London breweries by sailing barges, one of which is here seen loading its cargo in a photograph taken in about 1880 by George Christopher Davies. In the foreground are two wherries, a type of craft which traded throughout the waterways of North Suffolk and Norfolk; a third wherry with a new cloth in its sail is crossing the broad in the background.

Navigation on the rivers was rarely halted except by ice; even thin ice could be a serious hazard to wooden vessels. These six wherries are ice-bound in the New Cut near Haddiscoe Bridge in 1893. Even in such conditions some wherrymen managed to keep at work, for if their wherry were without cargo they would fill the hold with ice, to be delivered to one of the riverside icehouses as soon as the river was clear.

Until the coming of the railways a very large proportion of East Anglia's trade was carried on by sea. Coal from the collieries of north-east England came into Suffolk harbours or was landed on the beaches at Dunwich, Sizewell and elsewhere; grain grown on Suffolk farms went coastwise to other areas of the country; malt from the Suffolk maltings and flour from Suffolk mills went by sea to London; the foundries of Ipswich obtained their pig-iron by sea from South Wales; and a host of other cargoes were imported and exported in a multitude of small ships which crowded the narrow channels off the East Coast and all too often came to grief on the offshore banks.

Even hay and straw were carried by sailing barge from farms on the Orwell and Stour to the Metropolis to provide food and bedding for the horses on which London's transport depended. They returned with 'muck', the sweepings of those same stables into which their cargoes had been carried, which went to fertilize the Suffolk farmland.

Wherries traded regularly to Beccles, which was also reached by seagoing vessels by way of Mutford lock, Oulton Dyke and the Waveney. A timber yard, mills and maltings all made use of water transport. Seagoing ships were unable to negotiate Beccles bridge, but the wherries lowered sail and mast to pass the bridge and sailed on up to Bungay along a navigation dating back to the late eighteenth century.

Brigs and schooners, billyboys and barges helped to distribute the products of Suffolk farms and factories. When James Smyth at Peasenhall began developing a more efficient seed drill that was soon in demand from innovating farmers nationwide he offered to deliver them to the nearest port, from which the farmer was expected to collect them. As they were made at the Peasenhall works they were trundled off to Slaughden Quay for shipping.

With its mast lowered, a wherry lies on the Gillingham side of the river with the Beccles quays in the background. A number of wherries were built at Beccles by several generations of the Wright family.

Opposite. Beccles bridge was being rebuilt when George Christopher Davies took this photograph of a billyboy lying at the quay just below the bridge in August 1881. Beccles Corporation took advantage of the construction of Lowestoft harbour in the 1830s to improve the river so as to bring seagoing ships to the town, and for many years sailing coasters contributed to the town's commerce. In the 1950s there was a short-lived resurgence of maritime trade when a number of spritsail barges negotiated the Waveney with cargoes of grain for the town's flour mills.

The spritsail barges, which developed into powerful coasting vessels capable of voyaging not only around the coast but over to the Continent, were the last craft to trade under sail in northern Europe. Their easily handled rig, coupled with the labour-saving devices such as brail winches and leeboard winches with which they were equipped, made it possible for them to be sailed by a crew of two men, or two men and a boy in the largest vessels.

Many of the vessels that sailed from Suffolk ports were built in local shipyards. Those at Ipswich, particularly, played their part in the development of the sailing barge, launching not only spritties but also boomies and ketch barges that competed very successfully for many years with steamers in the North Sea trades.

To reach Bungay wherries passed through three locks, the first of which at Geldeston (or Shipmeadow) is seen here in the 1880s. The Bungay-owned wherry on its way upriver is clearly posing for the photographer, since normally the mast would be lowered when passing through the lock; there are bars at each end to prevent the wherryman from sailing his wherry into the lock, with the risk of colliding with the far gates.

In these two photographs the locks at Shipmeadow, above, and Ellingham, below, are seen under repair. In the picture above, a timber cofferdam is being constructed to enable the lock to be drained, and at Ellingham, below, the cofferdam is complete and the lock empty, revealing the sill of the upper gates.

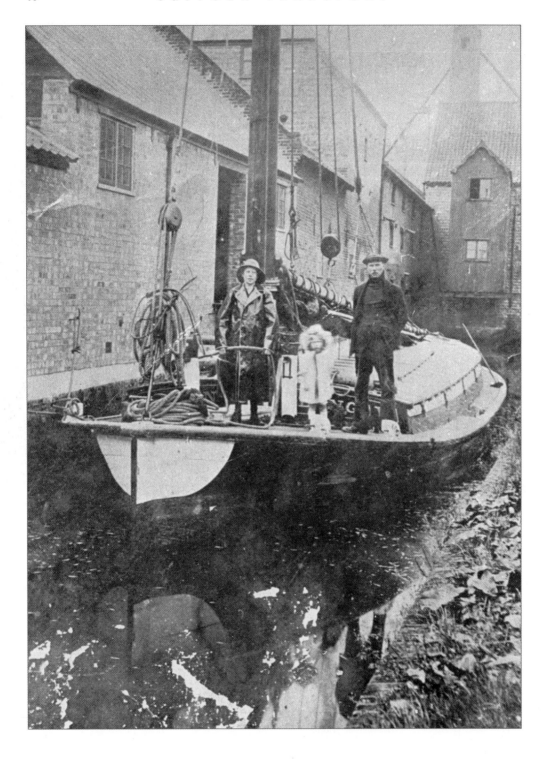

Wherries were also employed on the River Blyth between Southwold and Halesworth, replacing the keels that were used when the river was first made navigable in the mid-eighteenth century. Photographs showing trade on the Blyth are almost unknown, but this undated photograph of Southwold harbour looking across to Walberswick shows a wherry, with a transom stern, converted into a primitive dredger.

Opposite. Among the main wherry owners at Bungay were W.D. & A.E. Walker, millers and maltsters, for whom the *Albion* was built in 1898 by William Brighton. She is seen here at Bungay Staithe, the head of navigation on the Waveney. It was felt that a carvel-built wherry, with planks lying flush rather than overlapping, would be more satisfactory when working through the locks of the Bungay Navigation, so the *Albion* was the only trading wherry ever to be carvel built. She was taken over by the Norfolk Wherry Trust in 1949 after having spent a number of years as an unrigged lighter with Colman's, the Norwich mustard manufacturers, and is still sailing almost 100 years after her launching at Oulton Broad.

The billyboy ketch *Woodland Lass* at Blackshore Quay, Southwold, in the 1880s. Built at Yarmouth in 1851, she was typical of a numerous type of coastal carrier that served the small Suffolk ports throughout the nineteenth century. While many of the billyboys hailed from the Humber – their name is said to be derived from the nickname given to natives of Kingston-upon-Hull – a few were built in Suffolk yards, including the *Heart of Oak* launched at Southwold in 1836 and others from the Woodbridge yard. The billyboy could be taken as representing the coastal trader of the nineteenth century; the *Raybel* on the opposite page is typical of the sailing coaster of the first half of the twentieth, competing successfully with steam but having to give way eventually to other, more economical forms of power. The *Raybel* finished her life as a motor barge.

Alfred Sully's spritsail barge *Raybel*, a big coasting barge built at Sittingbourne in 1920, unloading a cargo of grain in Bass's Dock at Woodbridge. The grain was probably loaded from an ocean-going ship in the London docks; in the first half of the twentieth century a substantial part of the coasting trade was the distribution of imported goods brought into major ports, particularly London. Woodbridge was still quite a busy minor port in the 1920s, as may be judged by the number of craft in the picture; in the right background is a ketch barge, and almost hidden by the *Raybel* is a little billyboy ketch, possibly the *Mavis*, built of iron at Beverley in 1896 and owned at this period in King's Lynn. (Hugh Moffat)

The Dutch motor coaster *Magrietha* at Sun Wharf, Woodbridge, probably in the 1920s. The Dutch made great inroads into the British coasting trade following the decline of sail, British owners having few small vessels able to reach such berths as Sun Wharf, which was served by a horse-operated tramway from Woodbridge goods yard. It will be seen that while the *Magrietha* is a fully powered motor vessel she still carries sail; the wind was cheaper than fuel oil.

A trio of spritsail barges, one with its mast partly lowered, lying at Wilford Bridge, Melton, the head of navigation on the Deben, in the first decade of the twentieth century. There are stories of how ships once sailed up the river to Debenham, but it is certain that at least since the building of the bridge no seagoing ships have gone above this point. Below is George Mason's cement works at Waldringfield on the Deben, which was served by sailing barges bringing chalk from the Medway. The firm also had its own barge employed in supplying mud dug from the bed of the river at low tide.

Shipping in Ipswich Wet Dock, which was opened in 1842 when the mayor, John Chevallier Cobbold, passed through the entrance lock in the little sloop *Director* as it left for Rochester. In the foreground is the tiller-steered spritsail barge *Intrepid*, built at Ipswich in 1881, and backed up to the dockside as though to load freight from the *Intrepid* is a two-horse van belonging to Pickford & Company. (Ipswich Transport Museum)

The ketch barge *Ethel Edith*, built at Ipswich in 1892, in the lock at the entrance to Ipswich Dock with a number of spritsail barges, *c.* 1900. The large aperture in the wall of the dock to the left was the foundation for a swing bridge provided when the lock was constructed in 1879–81; the bridge was not built until 1903, when new railway tracks were laid down.

Overleaf. Shipping in Ipswich Dock in 1890, seen in a photograph by Charles Emeny, the Felixstowe photographer. On the left is a large vessel which has perhaps brought a cargo of barley from the Black Sea for the maltings that line the quay. In the middle of the picture a brig lies head to the quay by the oil mills, and on the right can be seen the stern of the Rochester spritsail barge *Challenger*, built on the Medway in 1875.

A number of barges can be seen in this view looking downstream from Stoke Bridge towards the mills and maltings around the Wet Dock. Both Cranfield Brothers, the Ipswich millers, whose premises can be seen in the middle of this view, and the maltsters R. & W. Paul had their own fleets of sailing barges operating right up to the 1950s, after which sails were replaced by diesel engines. The view below, looking in the opposite direction, shows trucks on the dockside tramway laid down soon after construction of the dock in the 1840s. The nearest barge, the *Aline*, was built at Ipswich in 1863 and owned at Harwich by William Groom, whose business interests included the operation of a sizeable fleet of barges.

Three of the Gipping barges belonging to Edward Packard & Co. Ltd under tow in the New Cut at Ipswich behind one of the firm's steam barges. Moored on the Stoke side of the Cut is the Great Eastern Railway's paddle steamer *Essex*. The Gipping barges worked between Ipswich Dock and the Packard artificial fertilizer works at Bramford carrying imported phosphate on the way up and manufactured fertilizer back. (Ipswich Transport Museum)

One of the Gipping barges can be seen lying alongside two coasting barges at St Peter's Dock, Ipswich, in the photograph above of Stoke Bridge, *c.* 1910. Edward Packard & Co. Ltd used the River Gipping to supply their works for many years, and were in fact the last users of the waterway. The picture below shows one of their steam barges, the *Trent River*, and another barge lying alongside the Bramford works; a dumb barge is emerging from the covered dock. (John Wilton and Ipswich Transport Museum)

Packard's steam barge *Trent River*, built by W.H. Orvis at Ipswich in 1916, on its way upriver with two dumb barges in tow. The 17-mile navigation, constructed under an Act of 1790 'for making and maintaining a navigable Communication between Stowmarket and Ipswich', was opened in 1793, almost immediately stimulating the growth of industry in Stowmarket. By the time this photograph was taken, however, barges had ceased trading to Stowmarket and Bramford was effectively the head of navigation on the river. (John Wilton)

For many years the Great Eastern Railway ran a steamer service on the Orwell between Ipswich and Harwich with the paddle steamers *Suffolk*, *Essex* and *Norfolk*. The *Essex* is seen above in the New Cut at Ipswich in Edwardian times with the *Woolwich Belle*, built for the Coast Development Corporation in 1891 by Denny of Dumbarton, which ran a feeder service between Ipswich, Harwich and Walton-on-the-Naze where it connected with the Belle steamers from London and Yarmouth. The picture below shows the *Norfolk* in the New Cut with the other river steamers.

The *Essex*, seen above steaming down the Orwell, was built by Earles Shipbuilding & Engineering Company at Hull in 1896; the slightly smaller *Suffolk* had come from the same yard a year earlier. The *Norfolk*, second steamer of that name to ply on the river, was built by Gourlay Brothers at Dundee in 1900; she is seen below arriving at Harwich pier. Two of the three steamers survived in railway ownership until 1931, but the *Essex* was sold by the Great Eastern in 1913. These three paddle steamers are still remembered with affection by the older generation of Suffolk people. (Ipswich Transport Museum)

The little farm barge *Cygnet* lying at her owner's quay in the Stour estuary in the early 1900s, seen in a photograph taken by Alexander Moffat. This tiny tiller-steered spritsail barge had been built at Frindsbury on the Medway in 1881, but for almost the whole of her life has been owned by members of the Wrinch family at Erwarton in the Shotley peninsula. In spite of her great age she is still to be seen sailing in local waters, now fitted with a wheel in place of the original long tiller. (Hugh Moffat)

Five River Stour lighters lying by the Anchor at Nayland at the beginning of this century, when the licensee of the Anchor was Thomas Goddard. The lighters carried cargoes between Mistley Quay and Sudbury until trade ceased on the river during the First World War. They were of similar design to lighters used on the Fenland rivers and worked in pairs or gangs using the second vessel to act as steerage to the first; no rudder was fitted. The 'tiller' was the long pole, seen here painted in red-and-white or black-and-white stripes, which extended from the bow of the second lighter and was loosely secured to the stern of the leading one.

Fenland lighters were employed on the Lark up to Bury St Edmunds and on the Little Ouse up to Brandon and Thetford. On the Little Ouse flash locks with guillotine gates known as staunches maintained a head of water for navigation; above is Brandon staunch. Alongside the river was a path known in this area as the haling path, haling being the local word for towing. Below, a number of lighters can be seen near the head of navigation at Thetford.

RAILWAYS

Two of the most successful engines employed on the Great Eastern Railway, which absorbed all the main lines in East Anglia on its formation in 1862, were the 0–6–0 tender engines of the Y14 class (LNER designation J15) and S.D. Holden's S69 (LNER designation B12) 4–6–0 express engines, the first six-coupled express passenger engines to run on the Great Eastern. Y14 No. 861 seen here was built in 1889; S69 No. 1535, for many years an Ipswich engine, came from Stratford Works c. 1912. (Ipswich Transport Museum)

One of James Holden's 'Claud Hamilton' class approaching Ipswich station over the Ancaster Road bridge with an up express from Norwich. The first of this class, No. 1900, was named *Claud Hamilton* after the GER chairman, and all the other unnamed engines of the class were thereafter known to railwaymen as 'Clauds'. (Ipswich Transport Museum)

The introduction of the 'rail road' to Suffolk was delayed by two false starts. The first proposal for a Norfolk & Suffolk Rail-Road Company in the 1820s with a proposed capital of a million pounds proved to be no more than an elaborate swindle. When the perpetrator, John 'Bubble' Wilks, died in 1846 the *Suffolk Chronicle* commented tartly that he had 'paid the debt of nature (the only liability he ever settled)'. And when the Eastern Counties Railway began building its line from Shoreditch to Norwich, which was to cross the Stour Valley on a ¾-mile viaduct 70 ft high just yards from Flatford Mill, the cash ran out and the line terminated at Colchester.

Nevertheless, Suffolk did get its first railways, from Colchester to Ipswich and from Ipswich to Bury St Edmunds, in 1846, with an extension to Norwich three years later. This was largely thanks not only to the determined efforts of Ipswich businessmen in raising the necessary cash but to the work of engineer Peter Bruff, who was responsible both for the construction of the Eastern Union Railway and for its operation when completed.

The hostility the Eastern Union encountered from the Eastern Counties Railway came to an end only when the ECR took over the working of the EUR in 1854. In 1862 the various railways in East Anglia were amalgamated into the Great Eastern Railway, which at the grouping of 1923 became part of the London & North Eastern Railway.

Throughout the years that the railways were spreading across the county they played a vital part in developing the local economy. Maltings and flour mills were attracted to the stations, sometimes being built on land owned originally by the railway company, and brickworks, lime pits and factories had sidings that fed traffic on to the main lines.

The railways also gave employment to large numbers of men and women. A job on the railway was a steady one, providing not only a regular wage but a certain prestige in the local community. It is not easy today, with a truncated railway system subject to a variety of political and social pressures, to realize just how great was the influence of the railways on the economy and the everyday life of Suffolk in bygone years.

A number of Suffolk brickworks had their own railway lines linked to the GER main line. The longest must have been that from the Woolpit Brick & Tile Company's works to the GER sidings at Elmswell, which operated in the early part of this century with two locomotives, a small 0–6–0 saddle tank called the *Jeanie* and the Sharp, Stewart tank *Haro Haro*, seen here with its crew. Built in 1870 for the Jersey Railway, the *Haro Haro* was employed on the Manchester Ship Canal construction lines before being purchased by the Woolpit Brick & Tile Company in 1902. (Woolpit Musuem P287)

Haverhill North station, *c.* 1870, looking towards Sudbury from the bridge over the Wratting road. Gravel ballast covers the sleepers, and there is a water column to supply water to the engines at the end of each platform. Later canopies were built over the platforms and a footbridge was erected to enable passengers to cross the line in safety. (Haverhill & District Local History Group)

Railway stations in even quite small towns had a large staff which included clerks, porters, shunters, a horseman to look after the shunting horses and those used for local deliveries as well as signalmen and others. Here, with the stationmaster in his place in the front row, are the staff of Haverhill North station in Great Eastern Railway days, probably not very long before the 1923 amalgamation that brought the London & North Eastern into being. There are twenty-seven men and women on the staff, yet Haverhill then had a population of no more than four thousand. When Haverhill became a London overspill town and the population soared the line was closed down under the Beeching Axe. (Haverhill & District Local History Group)

The Felixstowe Railway was opened in 1877 as an independent line, but only two years later the Felixstowe Railway & Pier Company entered into an agreement with the Great Eastern Railway for that company to operate the line. Above is the line's No. 1 *Tomline*, named after the company's chairman, George Tomline, and below is No. 2 *Orwell* with one of the coaches built for the line by the Gloucester Wagon Company.

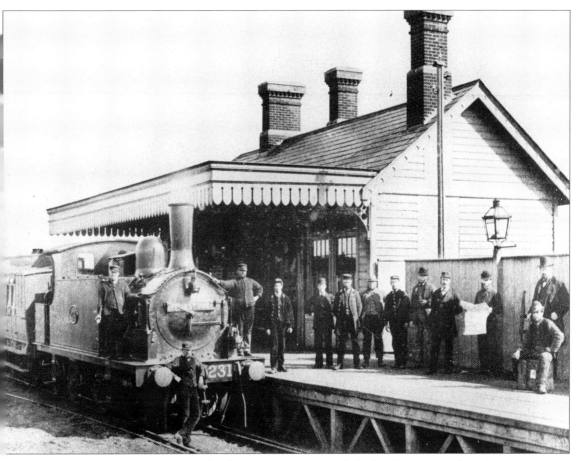

With the making of the agreement for the Great Eastern to work the line that company brought its own rolling stock on to the branch. This photograph taken by Charles Emeny in 1883 shows GER No. 231 at Felixstowe station; it is one of Massey Bromley's E10 class 0–4–4s, built at Stratford Works in 1880.

Orwell station on the Felixstowe branch, seen here as the light fades on a winter's day *c.* 1900, was George Tomline's own station, used for reaching his Suffolk home at Orwell Park. It is said that in the early days the station staff were dressed in Tomline's livery, but the legend that they were dressed as footmen in white breeches and silk stockings is probably no more than an embroidering of the original story. (Ipswich Transport Museum)

Trimley was not one of the original stations on the Felixstowe line but was opened in 1891 as the only intermediate station between Orwell and Felixstowe. Only one of the staff seen below wears uniform; the tall man third from left carries a conical oilcan with a flat base that was normal railway issue. (Ipswich Transport Museum)

Great Eastern class Y14 0–6–0 No. 545 at Ipswich, *c.* 1920. Engines of this class were first built in 1883, when they cost £1,300, and they lasted until the end of steam. Designed by T.W. Worsdell, these little engines proved highly successful, a total of 272 being built, all but 19 of them at Stratford Works. They were classified J15 by the LNER. Just to the right of the engine's safety valve is a mirror which enabled the signalman in the station box to see along the length of the up platform line. It was to have been removed on the introduction of track circuiting but signalman Jack Dolman prevented its removal and it proved its worth later when an old Manchester, Sheffield & Lincolnshire van used for engine spares was left on the line; the wooden Mansell wheels of this van meant that it failed to appear on the track circuit diagram in the box, and only a glance in the mirror enabled the signalman to avoid a disaster as an up train approached. (Ipswich Transport Museum)

The Mid-Suffolk Light Railway was to have run from Haughley Junction on the main Liverpool Street, Ipswich and Norwich line to Halesworth on the East Suffolk line, and also from Kenton Junction down to Westerfield. Work began in 1902, but the link to Halesworth was never completed, and passenger services terminated at Laxfield; goods trains went a little further to Laxfield mills. At Laxfield station in this photograph is the railway's No. 3, like its two compatriots an 0–6–0 built by Hudswell Clarke. (Ipswich Transport Museum)

Driver and fireman of N31 0–6–0 No. 978 pose not a little proudly for the photographer beside Long Melford Yard Box. They had some reason for pride, for they had a steady job at a time when many skilled craftsmen were liable to be laid off without pay if the weather prevented them from doing their work. The N31, known as the J14 after the grouping, had a higher pitched boiler and a bigger tender than the otherwise similar Y14 (J15 in LNER days). The turntable in the foreground might well have been made by the Ipswich firm of Ransomes & Rapier, who produced a high proportion of the turntables used on Britain's railways. (Ipswich Transport Museum)

On some lines trains were not all that frequent, and there was time for staff to enjoy a quiet game of draughts. The hours were long, however, their duties were many, and discipline among railwaymen was strict. (Ipswich Transport Museum)

The stationmaster makes an appearance in this photograph of the rail-served coal yard at Long Melford, above. In the background can be seen the large maltings built in 1878 by the Lion Brewery Company on land provided by the railway company. Horses long played their part in shunting work at Great Eastern stations, as seen in the picture below of two horses shunting wagons in the yard at Long Melford. The last shunting horse continued to operate at Diss until after the Second World War. (Ipswich Transport Museum)

Driver and fireman of M15 2–4–2 (later designated F4 by the LNER) No. 792 pose by the turntable at Long Melford. This engine was built at Stratford in 1886 and was not withdrawn until forty years later. Melford was a junction on the Stour Valley line just north of Sudbury; one line diverged towards Lavenham and Bury St Edmunds, while the Stour Valley line curved westwards and went through Clare and Haverhill to Cambridge. (Ipswich Transport Museum)

Railwaymen's pride in their job was apparent in the highly decorative gardens that became a prominent feature of many stations. An annual gardens competition was held for many years, the winning station being presented with a framed certificate recording its success. This garden at Long Melford features the station name laid out in whitewashed stones. (Ipswich Transport Museum)

Another part of the Long Melford station gardens, with the initials of the London & North Eastern Railway laid out in stone and plants. The inclusion of the ampersand in the initials suggests that these pictures date from the late 1920s. (Ipswich Transport Museum)

'Claud' No. 1832, seen here on an up passenger train at Ipswich, was one of the third series with Belpaire boiler and superheater, and with a wider cab than that fitted to earlier engines. Certainly the best known of James Holden's locomotive classes, the 'Clauds' first appeared in 1900 when No. 1900 *Claud Hamilton* was sent to the Paris Exhibition, where it earned a gold medal for excellence of workmanship, an international tribute to the high standards of Stratford Works. Engines of this class were still in service as the end of steam approached, but most unfortunately not a single example was preserved. (Ipswich Transport Museum)

A spotless S69 4–6–0 No. 1542 in the engine siding on the up side of Ipswich station. She was one of a batch of twenty of this class built by William Beardmore & Co. Ltd. in Glasgow in 1920–1, and had probably only recently entered service when this photograph was taken. Ipswich Station Box can just be seen above the buffer beam. Below is R24 0–6–0T No. 19 on the middle road at Ipswich, probably on its way to the Croft Street shed. Built in 1890 or 1891, this engine lasted until 1956. (Ipswich Transport Museum)

This unidentified S69 displays express headcode as it passes at speed through Manningtree station; it will very soon pass over the Cattawade viaduct into Suffolk. The calling-on signal by Manningtree Station Box enabled trains to be shunted into the yard on the left. Below is S69 No. 1563 at the head of an up passenger train standing at Ipswich. She was one of ten engines of this class built at Stratford in 1920. (Ipswich Transport Museum)

The signal gantry frames an S69 starting off a down express from Ipswich in the early 1920s. Faced with restrictions on weight because of the inadequate strength of some bridges on the Great Eastern, S.D. Holden had to keep the engine weight of the S69 down to 63 tons; the weight on the driving wheels, available for adhesion, was limited to 43½ tons. None the less, his design proved most successful, and in the hands of drivers from Ipswich Loco did some very fine work. (Ipswich Transport Museum)

A vital role was played by the men in the signal boxes, for the safe operation of the railway depended on their expertise and their memory. This is Ipswich Goods Junction Box a few hundred yards on the down side of Ipswich station. Below, inside the same box, can be seen the ranks of levers operating signals and points. The signalman's job was physically as well as mentally demanding, for it took considerable strength to pull over one of the levers. (Ipswich Transport Museum)

Permanent way workers at the beginning of the century, with portable forge and anvil for bending points rods. The man on the right is holding the handle of the bellows which blows up the forge. Below is a later photograph of a GER permanent way gang, with a piece of points rod heating in the forge. The bearing of the man third from left, with his hammer sloped over his shoulder, seems to indicate that he had seen service in the Army before joining the railway. (Ipswich Transport Museum)

The Great Eastern operated its own fire brigade at Ipswich, where this small steam fire pump mounted on a four-wheel flat truck was kept in a shed near the tunnel mouth reached by means of the wagon turntable seen in this picture, which was taken in 1911. The man seated in front of the fire engine is Fireman Sparkes, and Foreman Pennington appears in an inset portrait. Besides being used to deal with fires along the line the engine was sometimes taken off its rail truck and trundled to fires in the town of Ipswich, when the GER firemen worked alongside the Corporation firemen. (Ipswich Transport Museum)

Disaster struck on 25 September 1900, when the firebox of Y14 No. 522 collapsed at Westerfield. The boiler came to rest some distance away beside the level crossing. Both driver John Barnard and fireman William Macdonald died. By a tragic coincidence Driver Barnard's son, William Barnard, was one of those killed when S69 No. 1506 was destroyed in the Cromer express crash at Colchester in 1913. Also killed in the Colchester crash was fireman Sid Keeble, whose funeral at Ipswich is seen in the photograph below. (Ipswich Transport Museum)

Ipswich Goods Junction gave access to the yard on the other side of the Gipping in which this train is standing. The engine is GER T18 No. 292, an 0–6–0 tank built at Stratford Works in 1887, and the train is loaded with general service wagons constructed by Ransomes Sims & Jefferies for the Army in 1915. The line to the yard also gave access to the dock tramway that was laid down soon after the opening of the Wet Dock in 1842. (Ipswich Transport Museum)

A postman waits, leaning on his bicycle, as a goods train headed by what looks like a Y14 (LNER J15) passes through Brandon station. The staggered platforms resulted from the fact that this was where the Norwich & Brandon Railway linked with the Northern & Eastern, both lines being opened together in 1845. Both lines were taken over by the Eastern Counties Railway, which in its turn became part of the Great Eastern on its formation in 1862.

Every railway station of any real significance had its newspaper stand, operated by W.H. Smith & Son, who also delivered papers in the vicinity. Here is one of W.H. Smith's young employees with uniform cap and Raleigh bicycle equipped with pannier bags for carrying the papers. (Ipswich Transport Museum)

HORSES ON THE ROAD

A seaside holiday would hardly be complete without a trip by horse brake to some nearby beauty spot. This photograph of Royal Plain, Lowestoft, in the 1890s shows vehicles belonging to Henry Gage, who was born at Great Bromley in Essex in 1820 and settled in Lowestoft in mid-century. His business was passed on to his eldest son William and then to a grandson with the same name.

88 LOWESTOFT ADVERTISEMENT.

H. GAGE,

LICENSED TO LET

HORSES FOR HIRE,

CROWN HOTEL YARD,

LOWESTOFT.

BROUGHAMS, OPEN CARRIAGES,

Basket Phætons, Gigs, & Dog Carts.

Wedding Carriages, Hearse & Mourning Coaches

AT THE SHORTEST NOTICE.

₊ OMNIBUS AND CABS TO MEET ALL TRAINS.

William Gage and Sons were still operating as jobmasters when this photograph was taken of Lowestoft's Royal Plain in about 1910. The vehicles seen here plying for hire are for smaller, more select parties than the brakes.

Opposite. Henry Gage's advertisement from the 1860s, when he was operating from the yard of the Crown Hotel in Lowestoft High Street.

Until the development of the internal combustion engine the horse reigned supreme on the roads. Horses were ridden by the postboys who carried the mail from town to town; teams of horses took the prestigious stagecoaches on their journeys from one hostelry to another, the teams being changed at each stop; teams of heavier horses hauled the waggons on their slow travels from place to place; and it was horses that brought farm produce to market. Horses also powered the first trams and the omnibuses that collected passengers from railway stations and took them to their hotels, took the doctor on his rounds, and pranced between the shafts of the gentry's carriages.

Behind the horse was a great organization that supplied his fodder and his bedding, that arranged for his stabling, that saw to all his needs – even to the knacker who removed his body when he fell dead between the shafts. There were jobmasters who supplied both horses and vehicles as required, saddlers and harnessmakers, coachbuilders, wagon and cart builders, wheelwrights and farriers.

A hundred years ago there were no fewer than sixty jobmasters, fly and omnibus proprietors in Suffolk, and seven others listed in the directories as keepers of livery stables. From them horses, carriages and vehicles of all kinds could be hired, for weddings, funerals, or a day out at the seaside. Above, a party of customers from the Miller's Arms at the corner of William Street, Ipswich, one of the houses owned by Catchpole & Company of the Unicorn Brewery in Foundation Street, Ipswich, prepare for an outing, *c.* 1910. The two-horse brakes most likely belonged to Frederick Canham, whose stables were on the north side of St Matthew's Street, Ipswich. He also operated from the yard of the White Horse Hotel and from premises in Portman Road and Princes Street, and ran the Bath Stables in Bath Road, Felixstowe.

These two-horse brakes are taking men from the White Hart in Crowe Street, Stowmarket, on an outing at the beginning of the century. They would have been hired from a local jobmaster, possibly William Syer Ling, who was landlord of the Queen's Head in Station Road and also 'job and posting master'. Below is an 1892 advertisement for a Bury St Edmunds jobmaster. (Ivan Codd)

JAMES PETTITT,
GENERAL POSTING AND JOB MASTER,
LIVERY AND BAIT STABLES.

FUNERAL CAR & SHILLIBEER TO LET.
Mourning Coaches, Cab, Fly, and 'Bus Proprietor.
CORN, HAY, AND STRAW MERCHANT.

FURNITURE REMOVER & CARRIAGE BROKER.

ST. ANDREW'S STREET SOUTH, BURY ST. EDMUNDS.

Many hotels had their own omnibuses to meet people at the railway station. This one with its bowler-hatted driver is outside the Fox Hotel in Ipswich Street, Stowmarket. (Ivan Codd)

One of Canham's two-horse brakes outside the County Hotel in St Helen's Street, Ipswich, in 1912 with a party of men all in their Sunday best. Below is the Grundisburgh Brass Band in a rather less smart brake outside the premises of Robert Nunn, corn, coal and forage merchant, at Grundisburgh. Quite possibly the brake belonged to Robert Ablitt, who had livery stables in the village at the beginning of this century. (Ipswich Transport Museum)

Quite a selection of horse-drawn transport is to be seen in this photograph of A.A. Gibbons' West End Mills on the corner of Benezet Street, Ipswich, *c*.1905. In Benezet Street are two millers' wagons, one loading sacks of flour from a chute, the other already loaded; right on the corner is a coal lorry – Alfred Alexander Gibbons was described at this time as a 'miller & coal & general merchant' – and in Norwich Road is one of the firm's covered wagons with a pair of horses in the shafts. In the first decade of this century horses were universally used for deliveries, but within a few years firms such as Gibbons were using both steam wagons and motor lorries for this work. (Bob Markham)

A smart little turnout from George Abbott Ltd competing in a tradesman's horse show, *c.* 1912. The firm had an iron-works in what had been the Temperance Hall on the corner of High Street and Crown Street, Ipswich, and was described in a directory as 'stove & range & agricultural implement makers, builders' merchants, mechanical engineers & general machinists' – specialization had yet to come. Nevertheless, specialist vehicles did exist, such as those seen below which were used by Isaac Lord, maltster and corn merchant of 80 Fore Street, Ipswich, to distribute brewers' grains, the waste material left after brewing, used to feed cattle and pigs. (Bob Markham)

Buildings connected with horse transport still survive here and there. The Central Livery and Bait Stables built early in the twentieth century in Princes Street, Ipswich, still exist, though it is many years since any horses were baited there. For many years the building was home to Suffolk Seed Stores, as seen in this view.

Horses had an undoubted advantage when roads were flooded, as here in College Street, Ipswich, soon after 1900. Flooding in this area of the town was relatively common until the completion of a flood protection scheme in the 1970s.

Horse-drawn vehicles were made by craftsmen all over Suffolk. Herbert H. Spurden was landlord of the Crown Inn at Westhorpe, north of Stowmarket, for quite a few years from about 1915 onwards, and it would seem from this photograph that he combined this with a bit of dealing in wagons and farm implements. (John Wilton)

Reuben Earthy was a coach builder in Stowmarket in the 1850s, and according to the 1861 Census he was then employing 13 men and boys. When he died in 1873 his widow Mary Ann continued the business as Earthy & Sons with her sons William as manager and Alfred as foreman. For a period the firm also had a showroom in Stowmarket Market Place, seen here in about 1880. At some time in the 1880s or 1890s Alfred seems to have taken on the firm's original works in Bury Street and his mother moved to premises in Tavern Street, where she carried on business in her own name until her death in 1900. The West Suffolk Carriage Works, as the Tavern Street premises were known, were then taken over by John S. Plummer. The buildings survive, occupied now by a firm selling televisions and other electrical and electronic equipment. (Ivan Codd)

CHAS. HORSLEY & SON,
COACH BUILDERS AND HARNESS MAKERS,
(And for EXPORTATION), **BECCLES,**
67, And High St., Mary-le-Bone, London, W.
Carriages Jobbed at moderate charges, with option to purchase.

An advertisement of the 1860s for Charles Horsley & Son, of Hungate Street, Beccles, who were clearly in an extensive way of business. The two principals, Charles Horsley and his son Richard, both lived in Beccles, but they had premises in London which might well have served simply as showrooms. It is interesting to see that carriages might be jobbed, or hired, with an option to purchase.

IN TRADE

Firms like Oliver & Son, grocers, tea dealers, wine and spirit merchants and coffee roasters, of Abbeygate Street, Bury St Edmunds, who claimed to have been established in 1797 and had the Bury telephone number 1, used a variety of vehicles in their business. In this line-up, pride of place is taken by the traveller, with boater and gladstone bag, in his pony trap, with a smart two-horse wagon and other lesser vehicles behind. Standing beside the wagon are two delivery men with their trade cycles. (John Wilton)

Light vans such as these were used by many businesses for deliveries. These two belonged to the Tower Mill Steam Laundry in Bramford Road, Ipswich, which took its name from the brick tower windmill that stands in the background. The right-hand van has a wooden body; the other has wooden sides but a top of canvas stretched over a light wooden frame. Roundsmen of all kinds used horse-drawn carts of various sorts. The milkman seen below worked for Ernest Rush, of Chilton Hall Farm, Stowmarket, in the 1920s. (Ivan Codd)

Fruiterer Thomas H. Smith opened his shop at 66 Upper Orwell Street, Ipswich, *c.* 1890 and by early this century had extended to premises on the other side of the street. Like other tradesmen he made considerable use of horse-drawn transport. He is seen here, on the left, helping his sons to unload a consignment of oranges; by this time he was both a wholesale and retail fruit merchant.

Coalmen continued to use horse-drawn vehicles for deliveries long after motor lorries had come into use. This photograph of a cart belonging to R.B. Strickson & Son, of Stowmarket and Woodbridge, was taken after the Second World War, judging from the old Army greatcoat worn by the coalman, but Strickson had acquired a steam wagon at a much earlier period, as seen below. (Ivan Codd)

William Brown & Co. (Ipswich) Ltd used a variety of specialist vehicles in their trade of timber importers, cement manufacturers and builders' merchants. The one-horse lorry seen here was used to carry loads of tiles and similar goods to customers around the town; the driver had a board laid across from side-rail to side-rail to sit on when the vehicle was unladen. (Ipswich Transport Museum)

Traders used horse-drawn vehicles for delivery until the 1930s, and some continued to use horses until the 1950s. The fleet of vans seen on the previous pages was used for bread deliveries by the Ipswich Industrial Co-operative Society from their bakery in Cauldwell Hall Road, Ipswich.

Above is a horse-drawn greengrocer's cart owned by the Ipswich Industrial Co-operative Society, now the Ipswich & Norwich Co-operative Society. These were eventually replaced by a fleet of battery electric vehicles. (Ipswich Transport Museum)

Almost every business in every town required some form of transport, be it no more than a barrow or a bicycle for local deliveries. More extensive businesses had a fleet of vehicles from the trade cycle to the wagon, from the rep's pony and trap to the two-horse van.

House furnishers and removal contractors had bulky pantechnicons, and other trades operated specialist vehicles such as the pole waggons used by timber merchants whose wheelbase could be altered to conform to the load being carried and timber jims or jills employed to remove tree trunks from the woods to the sawmills.

Some large firms saw the advantages of steam haulage and acquired steam road engines or steam wagons such as those produced by Ransomes Sims & Jefferies at Ipswich and Richard Garrett & Sons at Leiston. These were, however, heavy and cumbersome, and the arrival of the petrol motor provided traders with a much more suitable alternative to the ubiquitous horse.

Charles Mayhew was operating as a carrier between Ipswich and Mistley, Manningtree and Colchester *c.* 1912. He regularly left the Coach and Horses in Upper Brook Street for the return journey at 4 p.m. every Tuesday and Friday. His van is typical of the vehicles used by the carriers, who after the First World War increasingly went in for motor vehicles; some survive until the present as bus operators. (Bob Markham)

Not everyone could afford a horse or pony, and there were many small tradesmen who 'crowded' their own barrows, to quote a piece of East Anglian dialect. A race for tradesmen with their barrows was a popular bank holiday event in Ipswich in the early years of the twentieth century, the course being from Great Colman Street out along the Woodbridge Road.

The Ipswich firm of Stammers & Son possessed a number of vehicles, including a pantechnicon used for household removals. Normally this was hauled by a pair of horses, but in the photograph above it is being towed by a Foden steam wagon. (Ipswich Transport Museum)

STAMMERS & SON,

❖ ## House Furnishers, House Agents, Removal Contractors & Storers,

6, 8, 10 & 12, Tacket Street, IPSWICH.

HOUSEHOLD REMOVALS

. . . By Road or Rail.

FURNITURE WAREHOUSED.

ESTIMATES   FREE.

FREE Register of Properties in Ipswich and its Neighbourhood to be Let or Sold

Illustrated Furnishing Catalogue Free on Application.

—— ESTABLISHED 1853. ——

David Hopgood was described at the beginning of his career as a general dealer; he travelled around the villages from his premises in Stowmarket selling oil, brushes and all the myriad items that householders might want to buy. At first he had the horse-drawn van seen above, but in the 1920s, by which time the business had become Hopgood & Son, hardware dealers, he acquired a motor vehicle to carry his wares. Sometimes, as seen on the opposite page, it appeared overburdened. (Ivan Codd)

Two Suffolk companies did a good deal to bring steam power to the roads. Ransomes Sims & Jefferies made steam wagons such as the one seen above ready for delivery to William Brown & Co. (Ipswich) Ltd, and similar vehicles were developed by Richard Garrett & Sons Ltd at Leiston. The Garrett tractor seen below at Thurston with two wagons in tow was possibly owned by Robert Downing, of nearby Norton, who combined farming with the business of haulage contractor, thrashing machine and steam plough proprietor. (Ransomes Sims & Jefferies, R.G. Pratt collection; Ken Leighton)

MOTORS ON THE ROAD

The very essence of early motoring is in this photograph of c. *1909, showing a Renault with a rear-entrance tonneau body. The East Suffolk registration provides a clue, but unhappily it has not proved possible to discover anything about the ownership or history of the vehicle. (Ipswich Transport Museum)*

Singer & Motor Cars.

SOLE SUFFOLK AGENTS—

A. F. GARNHAM & CO.,

Motor Engineers,

WOODBRIDGE ROAD, IPSWICH.

12/14 H.P. 4 Cylinders.

"SINGER"

FULL DESCRIPTIVE CATALOGUE ON APPLICATION of above, and
also 7/9 H.P. 2-Seated Model, 15 H.P. Touring Model, &c.

MOTOR REPAIRS.

CARS FOR HIRE by Day, Week or Month.

MOTOR TYRE REPAIRS.

Re-Treading and Re-Lining by Up-to-Date Process.

First-Class Workmanship.　　Moderate Charges.

Motor cars were still something of a novelty when A.F. Garnham & Co. produced this advertisement in 1908, though the Eastern Counties Automobile Club had been formed at Ipswich in 1903 and the West Suffolk Automobile Club was not far behind at Bury St Edmunds. Advertisers were not slow to take advantage of the car, as the picture below shows; Carreras Ltd used this car, seen outside James Lillistone's wholesale and retail tobacconists business in Station Road, Stowmarket, to advertise their Black Cat cigarettes. (Ivan Codd)

Overleaf. A car crosses the River Blyth by the steam chain ferry from Walberswick to Southwold, *c.* 1912. The River Blyth Ferry Co. was formed in 1885 to operate a chain ferry for vehicles, taking the place of the earlier rowing boat passenger ferry. (Ipswich Transport Museum)

William Clarke in Beach Road, Felixstowe, was an early hirer of cars, yet he continued to be described in directories as 'jobmaster' even in the 1930s. This photograph, used as an advertisement by 'Clarke's Motor Garage' *c.* 1912, shows a line-up of Unic cars. (Ipswich Transport Museum)

Because of the absence of windscreen and cab sides the driver of the first newspaper delivery van in Suffolk needed a waterproof coat, gloves and leather leggings to protect him from the weather. This vehicle came into use to deliver the *Evening Star* and the weekly *Suffolk Chronicle and Mercury c.* 1907.

The arrival of the horseless carriage heralded a revolution in transport that was to result in the decline of railways and the eventual construction of motorways. Such changes could have been foreseen by very few people when the first cars were imported into Britain in the 1890s from France and Germany.

The removal in 1896 of the requirement that any mechanically powered vehicle should be preceded on the road by a man carrying a red flag did little to ease the antagonism with which the upholders of the law regarded the motorist. There were few so far-sighted as a writer in the *Bury Free Press* who commented on the first Brighton run to celebrate the emancipation of the motor-car:

> The Brightonian quadrupeds are said to have greeted that draggle tailed remnant with
> a neigh of scorn, but all the same, we should be wrong to pronounce the motor car as
> a failure, or for a moment suppose it has not come to stay. It is in its callowest infancy
> at present, but it is destined to become a huge and mighty giant ere long. . . .

The growth of motor traffic at the beginning of the century led to many accidents. In Woodbridge, Horace Reynolds, known to all as 'Poll', became a voluntary traffic warden at the Cross Corner, a difficult junction in the town centre, and for almost three years directed traffic there. In 1910 he died of pneumonia at the age of thirty-two, but after a fatal accident at the corner a few months later a Mr Palmer took up the job of directing traffic there. It is Mr Palmer who is seen at work in this picture. In later years traffic was controlled by a policeman on point duty, seen below waving on a Tilling-Stevens petrol-electric bus on the Eastern Counties Road Car Company's No. 3 service to Melton. (Ipswich Transport Museum)

Reginald Egerton, one of the pioneers of the motor industry, joined an old-established coachmaking business in Ipswich in about 1902, but following a stormy disagreement he left that firm in 1910 and set up his own business in Northgate Street, Ipswich, 'adjoining Great White Horse Hotel'. These two photographs taken by Ipswich photographer Adolphus Tear in the 1920s show Buick cars in Egerton's showroom. (Ipswich Transport Museum)

Another Adolphus Tear photograph taken for Egerton's showing a Singer touring car, with an Ipswich registration. Reggie Egerton was well known to the local police in a period when motorists were a persecuted minority, and he was convicted on a number of occasions of such offences as exceeding the speed limit of 12 miles an hour and 'driving a motor car at a speed dangerous to the public'.

Two commercial vehicles supplied by Egerton's of Ipswich. Above is a truck supplied to the British Petroleum Co. Ltd and below is a Thornycroft operated by Ipswich millers Cranfield Brothers, photographed on the dockside near the firm's mills. (Ipswich Transport Museum)

In the 1920s Ipswich had a public vehicle battery charging station. Above is a van operated by Ipswich Corporation standing in Constantine Road outside the town's power station, and below is a Ransomes electric lorry belonging to Burton, Son & Sanders Ltd. (Ipswich Transport Museum)

A Straker–Squire articulated lorry with pneumatic tyres on the tractor front wheels and solid tyres on the other wheels, operated by Frasers (Ipswich) Ltd, and a Morris commercial van supplied in 1929 to Tollemache's Breweries Ltd for use by their wine merchant subsidiary, Barwell & Sons. (Ipswich Transport Museum)

George and James Cutting at Pettaugh Mills near Debenham had a sturdy solid-tyred lorry when this photograph was taken in the 1920s. The windmill was still working, but the main part of the business was a modern roller plant operated by a steam engine seen to the right of the windmill. Note the state of the road surface, and the puddles. (Ipswich Transport Museum)

In the nineteenth century Frederick Barnard was a posting master, with horses and traps for hire by the day, month or year, as well as being a fish salesman and beer retailer at the Norwich ale stores in Station Road, Stowmarket. Another member of the Barnard family was a bill poster. In the twentieth century Oliver George Barnard, jobmaster and bill poster, branched out by opening a garage in Station Road which is seen above. In the picture below, members of the Church Lads' Brigade set off for camp in one of Barnard's Ford lorries. (Ivan Codd)

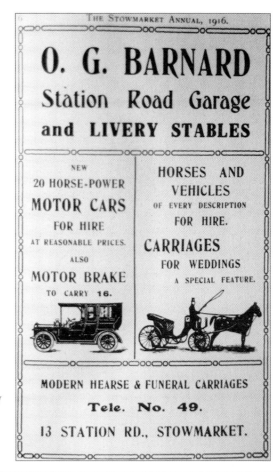

The advertisement on the right, dated 1916, shows O.G. Barnard as having horses and vehicles for hire, but already he has motor cars and a motor brake. Within a few years his firm was building coach bodies for fitting on a variety of chassis; below is a coach built for the Stonham and District Motor Service operated by Frank Elliott, carrier and grocer at Forward Green, Earl Stonham. (Ivan Codd)

By the 1930s new buildings were going up at the Stowmarket premises of O.G. Barnard & Sons. The company still thrives on the same site. (Ivan Codd)

PUBLIC TRANSPORT

Men of the Ipswich Corporation Tramways with the banner of the Ipswich branch of the Municipal and General Workers' Union. The electric trams came to Ipswich in 1903, replacing the horse trams which had operated since 1880. Trams also began running in Lowestoft in 1903. In 1926 Ipswich became the first town to replace its trams by trolleybuses, which had been introduced three years earlier.
(Ipswich Transport Museum)

Public transport in Ipswich dates back to 1880, when the first horse tramway line was constructed between the railway station and Cornhill, further routes following in succeeding years. This photograph of one of the Ipswich Tramways Company's double-deck trams, with bowler-hatted driver and the conductor sporting a boater, was taken in Derby Road station yard. Below is the horse tram depot in Quadling Street, which after the demise of the horse trams became a haulage contractor's depot; it has recently been cleared away for redevelopment of the area. (Ipswich Transport Museum)

A horse bus of the Ipswich Omnibus Service, set up in 1898. The 'Penny Omnibuses', as they were popularly known, not only provided competition for the horse trams but extended services into new areas. In spite of their nickname the board on the front of the bus reveals that the fare from Cornhill to the Ostrich at Wherstead, at one time a popular weekend resort for the townspeople, was 2d. (Ipswich Transport Museum)

As towns expanded during the Victorian period – between 1851 and 1901 the population of Ipswich more than doubled – there arose a need for a means of transport to get people to work, to the shops, and home again. Trams provided the answer to this need, first of all hauled by horses and then, at the beginning of the twentieth century, electric trams. Only two towns in Suffolk, Ipswich and Lowestoft, felt the need for tramway systems, and in Ipswich the trams gave way in the 1920s to the 'trackless tram', the trolleybus.

In the countryside the arrival of the motor bus, at first promoted by the railway company and later by a host of small concerns, brought about a social revolution that is only being studied now that bus services are contracting, faced by almost universal car ownership.

An Ipswich Tramways Company double-deck tram on the Cornhill. In the background can be seen the premises of William Claridge & Co., saddlers and harness makers, whose premises were later demolished to extend the shop of John Henry Grimwade & Son, tailors. (Ipswich Transport Museum)

Ipswich Corporation compulsorily purchased the horse tram system, which had never proved a financial success, in 1901 and the horse trams ceased running in June 1903, so that the old rails could be lifted and new ones for the electric trams laid. Here men working on the construction of the new tram track and the tram depot at Constantine Road pause for the photographer in the summer of 1903. The depot is used today by Ipswich Buses. (Ipswich Transport Museum)

A scene of great activity as the horse tram lines are lifted from Cornhill in 1903 preparatory to laying the rails for the new electric trams. The horse trams had ceased running on 6 June; public services using the electric trams commenced on 23 November, though only one route was then open. (Ipswich Transport Museum)

Men of Ipswich Corporation Tramways outside the Constantine Road depot in the early days of the undertaking. In the picture are three of the twenty-six cars ordered from Brush Electrical Engineering Co. Ltd of Loughborough in 1903; the electrical equipment was supplied by the Westinghouse Company. A further ten cars were ordered from Brush the following year. (Ipswich Transport Museum)

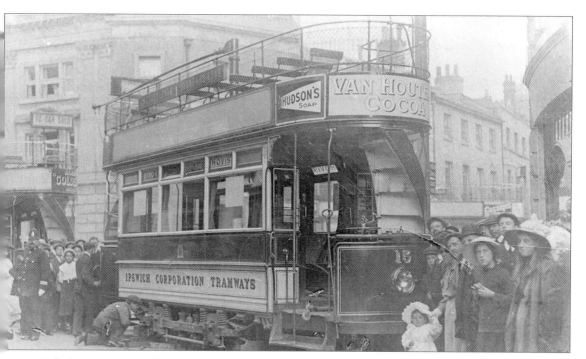

Onlookers are attracted by the spectacle of car No. 15 derailed at the junction of Princes Street and Queen Street. Such mishaps became more frequent as the track became worn, particularly as the First World War led to maintenance being neglected. (Ipswich Transport Museum)

Opposite. The driver and conductor of car No. 3 pose for the camera at Derby Road before beginning the return journey to Whitton. The driver has a metal 'Motorman' on his cap, the conductor the word 'Conductor'. (Ipswich Transport Museum)

Overleaf. Work in progress at the junction of Princes Street and Friars Street in 1924 to lift the tram rails and resurface the road. Trolleybus No. 2, one of three obtained from Railless Ltd of Rochester, is on its way from the station to Cornhill; T.W. Peart's motorized carrier's cart has little room to pass. (Ipswich Transport Museum)

Under the Great Eastern Railway (General Powers) Act of 1904 the GER obtained powers to run buses, and in that year it began a service between Lowestoft and Southwold, providing competition for the legendary Southwold Railway which ran between Halesworth and the seaside town. The following year a service was started between Ipswich station and Shotley, and in 1908 new routes between Bury St Edmunds and Horringer and Bury and Stanton were brought into operation. This photograph shows one of the Maudslay buses operating on the Bury–Horringer route at Bury St Edmunds station; the board on the side bears the old name for Horringer, 'Horningsheath'.

Worried by the cost of the first buses, the GER built a number of buses for itself at Stratford Works. It is one of these that is seen above at Ipswich station, about to depart for Shotley. The railway company also obtained three Thornycroft vehicles in 1905, and one of these with the East Suffolk registration BJ-416 is seen below at Lowestoft; it has been fitted with a charabanc body, perhaps for summer use only.

Electric trams operated by Lowestoft Corporation began running in the summer of 1903 and continued in service until 1931. The gauge was 3ft 6in, the same as the Ipswich tramways, and only about a third of the 4-mile route was double track. Special arrangements had to be made for the crossing of the swing bridge over the harbour, in the background of the picture above of London Road North. In High Street there was a length of interlaced track, seen below, which in operation could hardly have been superior to single.

A bus driver of the 1920s: Reg Chatterley of the Eastern Counties Road Car Company, a concern set up in the southern part of the county in 1919. It was absorbed into the Eastern Counties Omnibus Company in 1931. (Ipswich Transport Museum)

Buses of United Automobile Services outside Lowestoft station in the 1920s. The nearer vehicle is on the No. 4 service between Lowestoft and Kessingland Beach. Formed in 1912, United went on after the First World War to convert ex-army lorries into buses, thus founding what in time became Eastern Coach Works. United was also absorbed by the Eastern Counties Omnibus Company in 1931.

An Eastern Counties Road Car Company bus crew with their Tilling–Stevens bus in the Market Place at Southwold. The destination board is typical of those used by ECRCC, with the route number superimposed on the place names. Below is a scene on the Cornhill at Ipswich in the late 1920s, with an elderly roadsweeper working among the trolleybuses. (Ipswich Transport Museum; East Anglian Film Archive)

Driver Creswell and his conductor with their Eastern Counties Road Car Company bus outside the GPO Sorting Office in the Old Cattle Market at Ipswich in the 1920s. No route number is displayed on the destination board, which reveals that they were bound for Stowmarket, via Claydon and Needham Market. A development of the metal destination board was the 'tin bible' used by the Eastern Counties Omnibus Company which had a hinged section that could be turned up and clipped in position for the return journey; there are examples of 'tin bibles' in the Ipswich Transport Museum collection. (Ipswich Transport Museum)

Eastern Counties Road Car Company conductor No. 136, Fred Simpson, seen in a portrait taken in 1929. He worked with driver Reg Chatterley, seen on page 121. (Ipswich Transport Museum)

Frank Fisher and Fred Simpson with their Leyland TD1 on the Stowmarket run in the summer of 1930. In hot weather ECRCC staff were provided with light white coats and white cap covers. (Ipswich Transport Museum)

This late-1920s photograph by Frederick Gillson of Felixstowe Road, Ipswich, shows a Tilling–Stevens double-decker of the Eastern Counties Road Car Company on the No. 7 route to Felixstowe. In the background can just be seen an Ipswich Corporation trolleybus on its way into town. Below are two buses in the scarlet and cream livery of the Eastern Counties Omnibus Company in Stowmarket Market Place in the early 1930s. Could the smaller vehicle be that seen in Road Car Company colours on page 123? (Ipswich Transport Museum; Ivan Codd)

With the coming of the Second World War women not only became 'clippies' as they had in the earlier war but took the driving seat on the trolleybuses in Ipswich. By this time the metal cap badge says 'Driver', in place of the earlier 'Motorman'. (Ipswich Transport Museum)

BRITAIN IN OLD PHOTOGRAPHS